i

Foreword by Pastor Karen Smith

In The Midst of Revival

from glory to glory...
2 Corinthians 3:18

Michelle Lamb

In The Midst of Revival

Cover design by: Marty Darracott

Author photo by: Kati Simpson

Copyright 2023 by Michelle Lamb

ISBN: 9798862505689

Printed in the United States of America

2023 - First Edition

In loving memory of Aunt Becky and Baby Oliver

TABLE of CONTENTS

Dedication

A huge thank you to Pastors Todd and Karen Smith of Christ Fellowship Church in Dawsonville, Georgia, and home of the North Georgia Revival! Thank you for your hunger and obedience to the Lord. Pastor Todd, thank you for finding the dark, seeking Him with everything, and dying that day. Thank you for showing us how to live a holy, purified life unto the Lord and for shepherding us so well. Pastor Karen, thank you for feeding my hungry soul with truth and passion. My family honors you both for your leadership and impact in our lives.

I want to thank my husband. You are my biggest cheerleader. You believe in me even when I don't. You will never know how much your support means to me. I am so thankful to be by your side and that we get to do what we do for Him, together. Thank you for leading us so well.

To my beautiful and loving mom. You have always encouraged me to try anything and everything. You have taught me to never fear stepping out of my comfort zone and trying something new. You keep me grounded and remind me how to love and show kindness to every person I meet. Thank you for being a wonderful example of a humble and loving person.

To my dad for instilling in me the truth that I can accomplish anything if I put my mind to it, and for being that example for me my whole life. I will always be your baby girl!

To my two amazing children and their families: You will never know just how much you mean to me. My heart overflows with love and joy because the Lord has blessed me with you and your growing families. Never give up on your dreams no matter how much time has passed by. When you fall, get back up, dust off your knees, straighten your crown, remember who you are in Jesus Christ, and go at it again. If you quit trying, you will fail for sure.

Finally to my mother-in-love: You are my fearless intercessor! I would not be where I am today without your fearless and faithful prayers. I am thankful God chose you for me.

Introduction

Ever since I was a little girl, I have loved reading and writing. English/Composition was my favorite subject in school. I can remember feeling the excitement on the inside when my teacher would give us a writing assignment. It didn't matter what we had to write about; I was the most excited kid in the class! I remember being so anxious to get home and start on the assignment.

My secret dream of being an author eventually faded away as the busyness of life took over. I had convinced myself many years ago that it was one of those silly childhood dreams. I heard the enemy whispering in my ear that I had messed up my life so much that I wasn't good enough to write anything. However, the Lord renewed my love for writing during my first year of Bible college back in 2017.

In my early forties, I took a short four-week summer class at KINEO Ministry Training Center on Holy Spirit. This class created an unquenchable hunger within me to know more about Him. A week or so after this class ended, I registered for the year-one course at the training center. When asking questions to the instructor about the class, Pastor Karen Smith looked at me square in the face and simply said, "It will change your life."

Little did I know how much this class would change not only my life but the life of my family! Revival started during my first year of KINEO and **marked** me for life.

I have spent much time in prayer and spiritual warfare to write this book over the last twenty-four months. It is my heartfelt prayer that it will bring revelation to you about Him and how we must alter our lives in order to give Him more room to move and do what only He can do. It is my firm belief that we will see Him return for us in our lifetime. I know that's a bold statement, but it has been on my heart since my childhood. It is time to stop playing church and BE the CHURCH that He died for. It is time for His Bride to cleanse herself and prepare the way. It is time for Him to receive the FULL REWARD for His sacrifice for us!

I pray that this book will encourage you to seek the Lord for His truth, ALL of His truth! I pray that this book will encourage you to have a true, meaningful relationship with Him. I pray that you see that He is not angry with you and all He wants is *everything.* He wants all of your heart — every piece of it. He wants all of your failures, all of your struggles, all of your dreams, all of your desires. He wants it all. Jesus gave up everything for you! He is the One who carries your guilt, the One who carries the shame that no one knows about. When you feel as if you have made too many mistakes for the Lord to still love you and want you, He carries your unworthiness. **He deserves everything**!

He came for you. He came so that you would have hope — through Him — in this lost and fallen world. He is our light. He is our hope. He is the only One who can cleanse us and make us whole. We were created to have a relationship with Him. YES! The Creator of the universe wants a relationship with you! That is the missing piece in each and every person's life. The longing for your Creator was deposited inside of you at your conception! You are worthy to Him. He has already paid the price for you. Reach out to Him and receive His salvation, His redemption, His healing, His cleansing, His hope, His love, His peace, His joy, His mercy, His grace, and His will for your life. He is worthy of it all. All of you for all of Him!

Foreword

I remember one of the first times I spoke with Michelle at our church, Christ Fellowship, in Dawsonville, Georgia. I remember her quiet spirit, her gentle smile, and the grace with which she entered the room. But more than anything else, I remember her hunger and intrigue to know more about the One called Jesus!

It didn't take much to convince her to become a part of our Bible school, KINEO Ministry Training Center under my instruction. Her first class was a study on the Holy Spirit and that led to her enrolling in the four-year program. The more she learned, the more she wanted to learn! The LORD took every, "Yes!" she said to Him and He gave her more and more in exchange. Over the course of time, she and her husband Jason, fell deeper and deeper in love with the LORD. He solidified His love for her in her heart and He answered the questions she had asked for so long. I saw her settle into a level of peace that only comes from *truly knowing Him!*

Since then, she has experienced Him in the waters of revival and she values the privilege of serving others as they, too, meet Jesus in the water. Michelle is a pillar in our church and an intricate part of the North Georgia Revival. Her testimony is a shining example of what total surrender to Jesus will do in a person's life. Enjoy her book, *In the Midst of Revival,* and know she wrote her story from experience. She has seen Him move in undeniable power and she has hosted His glorious presence. The change in Michelle's life and the fulfillment she found in Jesus is available to everyone, to everyone who says, "Yes," to Him. May her story create a hunger in you to know Him like she does!

Dr. Karen L. Smith
President, KINEO Ministry Training Center
Christ Fellowship Church
Dawsonville, Georgia

Testimony

When I look at my friend, Michelle Lamb, I see a woman of strength. I see a woman who has overcome many obstacles in her life and has done so with a tenacity that most simply do not have. I have watched as she has handled overcoming addiction. I have watched as she has handled grief. I have watched as she has fully given herself to the Lord during her time at Christ Fellowship Church, and have noticed a transformation in her. Bottom line is that she has changed. She has changed from a woman who lived in fear to a woman who is full of faith. She has changed from a woman filled with insecurities to a woman who fears nothing because she knows her identity in Christ. I have watched her as she transformed from a quiet, meek person to a woman full of humility…the kind of humility that gives strength.

Do you have unfilled desires in your life? Do you have unmet dreams and aspirations? Do you have unspoken fears or sin in your life? Do you have a desire for the things of God but simply do not know how to tap into them? Michelle Lamb's *In the Midst of Revival* is her story of how God took an ordinary woman and transformed her into a woman clothed in strength and dignity.

You, too, can have this life-changing transformation. Read Michelle's story of how the North Georgia Revival has changed her life into something worth living! Be inspired that He who began a good work in you will carry it on to completion until the day of Christ (Philippians 1:6). He will revive all the dark places in your life.

As we say at the North Georgia Revival, "Jesus, send the fire."

Dana Fowler

Chapter 1: The Encounter

Psalm 40:1-3 NIV

I waited patiently for the LORD;
he turned to me and heard my cry.
He lifted me out of the slimy pit,
out of the mud and mire;
he set my feet on a rock
and gave me a firm place to stand.
He put a new song in my mouth,
a hymn of praise to our God.
Many will see and fear the LORD
and put their trust in him.

In September 2017, I began my journey as a KINEO Ministry Training Center Year I student. I was hungry for truth.

In July of that year, I had taken a short, four-week class on Holy Spirit, and what I learned about Him blew my mind. I had never been taught about Holy Spirit and how He works through us. I knew who Jesus and Father were, but I didn't know much about Holy Spirit, and how He works in the Trinity.

I still had some doubts on the Bible concerning its accuracy, truth, etc. I am a little left-brained so I have to have details. Lots of details! I can't always accept someone else's word or interpretation. I have to understand the "why" and "how." I have to do my own research and learn for myself. I have to know that I know.

My entire life I had always wondered where the "God of the Bible" was. Why doesn't God do great things today like He did in the Bible? Were the events in the Bible even true? How could I know for sure? Where was the power demonstrated in the Bible? How could I believe the testimony of a "witness" in the Bible since it seems like the honor of being a witness is taken so lightly today? This Year I class introduced me to the New Testament and gave me the answers that I had searched for my whole life.

The North Georgia Revival started a few months prior to graduation, and I was amazed at what I was seeing. I had never experienced anything like that before. It only made my hunger for Him that much greater. I had witnessed over and over again people getting touched in almost indescribable ways, both at the altar and in the baptismal waters. I had felt His presence several times during those few months at the altar and even in my seat when I was too fearful to go to the altar. Feeling His presence is extremely hard to describe with words. I can only describe it as a feeling of heaviness. Take a moment and imagine an invisible cloud physically pressing down on your body. With each passing moment, the weight gets heavier and heavier. The inward conviction of your sin and the poor state of your soul presses you to the floor until you are face down, begging for forgiveness and mercy from the One who created you. Your soul immediately recognizes the presence of the Holy One. There is zero room for doubt or debate. The sense of awe and wonder fill your mind, body, and soul. Your soul knows and recognizes its Creator without any input from your flesh.

In June of 2018, my hunger for Him was even greater than it was at the beginning of the school year. I had eagerly searched for Him and met Him during the school year. Matthew 7:7 (NIV) tells us, "Ask and it will be given to you; seek and you will find; knock and the door will be opened to you." The Lord does not hide Himself from us! When we seek Him, He reveals Himself in powerful, mighty ways to each one of us. The world has so many distractions to keep us from seeking Him with all of our heart.

Just a week after my Year I graduation, I had a life-changing encounter with Jesus as I was baptized in the waters at the North

Georgia Revival.

I didn't have any hesitations about receiving from the Lord. We had been living in the visitation from the Lord for several months. While I didn't know exactly what to expect when I got in the water, there was zero fear. I knew I could trust Him. I had spent nine months in a classroom devouring every piece of information I could get to learn if He was real or not. He had revealed Himself to me throughout the year. He had reaffirmed that He was the Creator. He had reaffirmed that He *loved* me. He had shown me forgiveness with my repentance. He had taken this broken and lost woman and turned her into a confident, restored daughter. I had complete peace and a lot of expectation.

When I got into the water, I asked Him for my exchange. I finally understood what my Salvation meant. I finally understood the depth of what He did for me on the cross, and I was ready for the exchange. I wanted to uphold my end of the covenant and to receive what Jesus paid for me on the cross. I could already feel His presence. I was weeping before I got into the water. I went under the water and came back up. I tried raising my arms (they felt heavy and I don't think they moved very much) and silently told the Lord that I wanted more of Him. I knew there was more! I had seen people experience Him in powerful ways in the baptismal water, and I wanted ALL He had for me! I silently told Him I wasn't leaving the water until I knew without a doubt that I had received all that He had for me.

As I was asking the Lord for more, I remember Pastor Marty putting his hand on my forehead. I do not remember anything he said, but I distinctly remember hearing the word "fire." The next thing I knew, I was trying desperately to hang on to the side of the pool and not slip under the water! I felt as if I had been given anesthesia. As someone who has had nine surgeries, I know exactly what the effects of anesthesia feel like. This is the best description that I can give to try to explain how I felt. I could not move my arms or any part of my body easily. I was so weak and every limb felt like it weighed a thousand pounds. I felt "out of it" mentally. I didn't feel any fear. I never felt threatened or that I was in danger. It is hard to describe because it was such a supernatural experience. I felt nothing but security and love. It was as if His love – to its fullest sense – had wrapped around my body comforting my soul in every possible way. It was so peaceful and unexplainable.

I could not immediately remember what happened until I realized I was still in the water and sitting on one of the exit steps. When I "came to," I remember thinking that I must be holding people up from going home. I had no idea what had happened or how long I had been "out." Somehow, I knew that I did not have a medical emergency but that it was the Lord. I could still feel His presence.

I made my way up the steps and climbed out, gradually making my way to one of the changing rooms. I was moving slowly and with great care with every step I took. I felt heavy and disoriented. Once I was inside the private room, I was on my knees and crying uncontrollably. I could still feel the weight of the Lord's presence upon me, and all I could do was weep. I was being cleansed from the inside out. Somehow, I knew He was reaching down to all the dark, hidden, hurt places in my heart, clearing out all the shame and guilt I had carried my whole life. He replaced every single remnant of darkness that I still carried: shame, guilt, pride, doubt, fear, hopelessness, anxiety. He wiped away every question I had about His existence--how real He is; whether or not He still loved me since I had made so many mistakes in my life.

This encounter with the Lord marked me for **LIFE**. I am forever grateful for His grace and mercy. I am forever changed by His love and the encounter I had with Him in the water. I now have a boldness for His truth that I never knew was possible. I now have a love for Him and His truth that I never thought could exist. He has revitalized my life and my dreams. He has brought new meaning and purpose to my life. He has deposited a fire within me that I will carry for the rest of my life.

This is my experience and what I have learned about hosting His presence in the midst of revival. I did not grow up in a Spirit-filled church, and I didn't receive the Baptism of Holy Spirit until about two months prior to the revival starting. I had a great deal to learn about repentance, forgiveness, deliverance from pride, self-hate, self-doubt, and fear. I had a great deal to learn about how to live humbly before the Lord daily. I had to learn how to honor Him in all that I do. Did you know that you can grieve Him? I never want to grieve Him again! Ever. If I do something that does grieve Him, I promptly respond to Holy Spirit's nudging and repent quickly. My heart posture is to listen to Holy Spirit and yield to Him so that He can teach me how to be more like Him every single day.

I do not fully understand why the Lord has chosen water baptisms for this revival. As I learned more about our Jewish heritage and the history of water in the Bible, it began to paint a picture of Jesus washing His Bride and cleansing her. Most modern-day Christians have forgotten to preach the full Truth of

His Word. We have lost our love for our Savior, and we have normalized sin. Most of the time, it is hard to tell the difference between a "Christian" and a "non-believer." One would wonder why you would need to question Father's plan for water baptisms with the abundance of sin we have accepted as "normal" and "okay" and even allowed within the Church. Our Savior will not return to a blemished Bride but to one who is clean, pure, spotless, and holy. He will not return for a "worldly" Bride. He will only return for a sanctified Bride.

Chapter 2: What is Revival?

Psalm 63:1

You, God, are my God,
earnestly I seek you;
I thirst for you,
my whole being longs for you,
in a dry and parched land
where there is no water.

"A necessary pre-cursor of any great spiritual awakening is a spirit of deep humiliation growing out of a consciousness of sin, and fresh revelation of the holiness and power and glory of God."

John R. Mott

Dictionary.com gives these definitions of the word "revive": to activate, set in motion, or take up again; renew; to restore to life or consciousness; to return to life, consciousness, vigor, strength, or a flourishing condition.

In order to revive something, it must first have had life. Let's read that again: in order to revive something, it must first have had life. How do you apply that to your spiritual life? Let's look at our history for a better understanding.

When Adam fell in the Garden, he essentially became "dead" to God. It doesn't mean that his physical body fell over and died that instant. Adam actually lived to be 930 years old. It does mean that he was now spiritually separated from God due to sin (the result of eating the forbidden fruit). Adam could no longer be in the presence of God as he had been since he was created. Now he was spiritually unclean and separated from God's presence. Mankind needed to be redeemed in order to spiritually fellowship with the Lord again in His presence. Enter Jesus and His perfect plan of redemption!

Jesus redeemed us through His death on the cross and resurrection. We can now have a one-on-one relationship with Father God again. We no longer need the sacrifice of bulls and goats to cover our sin. We no longer need one man to enter the Holy of Holies, one day a year, to cover the Mercy Seat with the blood from the sacrifice of an animal to atone for our sins. Jesus's work on the cross was complete and covers our sin forever. If you study the tabernacle in the Old Testament, you will understand why the veil was torn the instant Jesus gave up His Spirit to Father while hanging on the cross. Jesus replaced that veil with Himself. He is now the one and only path for us to have a direct relationship with Father God again.

When we get saved, we may "feel" God touch us and experience a mixture of emotions like relief, happiness, contentment, hope, joy, and love. But check back in a few weeks or a few months or even a year. What happened? Where did that joy go? Where did the happiness go? Why do you feel like Satan is running you over day in and day out? Why are you still fighting your old sin pattern? Why do you feel defeated every time you turn around? What happened to your commitment to prayer time? Where did your enthusiasm go for studying His Word? Guess what? Your spiritual walk with Father God now needs reviving!

Revival is essentially a spiritual awakening in a dry, spiritually lifeless person or church. It is an awakening of the heart, mind, and soul to the true nature and wonders of the Lord. It is an increased passion and devotion of one's self for the ways of the Lord. It is an increased awareness of His presence. It is an increased awareness of your *need* for Him. It is readjusting your schedule to spend more time with Him. It is a fire burning within that cannot be quenched by anything except His presence. It is a realization that you can no longer watch the movies you used to watch, say things you used to say, or do things you used to do. It is an ever-present awareness that what you think, say, and do either brings honor to the Lord or it grieves Him. This awakening of your heart leads you to want to please the Lord in all that you do. It also brings a newfound hate for sin in your life and the lives of others. It brings a new level of commitment and boldness for righteousness. It brings a new level of prayer, fasting, and devotion to your life. It brings a whole new level of gratitude for all that He has done.

The Lord longs for a spirit-filled body that takes Him at His Word. He longs for people that will put Him above everything else in their life. He longs for a relationship with each and every person, just like your relationship with your spouse or best friend. He longs to have you believe Him and His Word. He longs for you to trust Him in every area of your life. He longs for you to give Him the opportunity to show you how good He is. He longs for you to stop trying to do everything on your own. He longs for you to stop leaving Him out of your life. He longs for you to go out into the world to show the unbelievers who He is. He longs for you to love each and every person because they mean everything to Him. He longs for the world to see and know Him. He is not a past-tense God. He is not a God of yesterday.

He still sits on the throne. He still reigns! He is still moving and working today as much as He was one, two, or even five thousand years ago. He longs for His Bride to walk in the power and authority for which He died. He wants to return to His Bride, so we must yield ourselves to Holy Spirit and prepare the world for His return.

I love this quote by Billy Sunday: "When is a revival needed? When carelessness and unconcern keep the people asleep." And this one by Andrew Bonar: "Revivals begin with God's own people; the Holy Spirit touches their heart anew, and gives them new fervor and compassion, and zeal, new light and life, and when He has thus come to you, He next goes forth to the valley of dry bones… Oh, what responsibility this lays on the Church of God! If you grieve Him away from yourselves, or hinder His visit, then the poor perishing world suffers sorely!"

Psalm 85:6 (NIV) says, "Will you not revive us again, that your people may rejoice in you?"

Believe it or not, America has a deep history of revival. There were times where whole cities would shut down to attend an evening or mid-day prayer service. Businesses would close so that employees could attend the prayer services. Taverns would shut their doors due to a lack of patrons.

Revival was brought from England to America in the 1730s by the Wesley brothers, Charles (1707-1788) and John (1703-1791), and also by George Whitefield (1714-1770). This era is known as the Great Awakening and lasted from approximately 1734-1743.

The revivals in New England began in the late 1700s and spread through Connecticut, Massachusetts, New York, and Kentucky. This wave of revival lasted up until the 1840s and is known as the Second Great Awakening (1790-1840). Below is a list of a few other revivals that have occurred here in the United States and around the world:

*Korean Revival (1903-1907)

*Welsh Revival (1904-1905)

*Azusa Street Revival (1906-1909)

*Hebrides Revival (1949-1953)

*Jesus Movement (1967-1972)

*Brownsville Revival (1995-2000)

*North Georgia Revival (February 2018-Present)

Jesus WANTS revival! Jesus wants us to make Him the center of our lives again. And not just our personal lives. He wants to be the center of our families, our churches, our businesses, our finances, our schools, our homes, our football games, our soccer games, you name it! He wants to be the LORD of our lives in every aspect. He wants to show us His goodness. He wants us to be dependent on Him and to stop trying to do everything ourselves. He wants to take care of us. He wants to provide all of our needs. He wants to bless His children! He does not want us to go without. He is a God of abundance. He is a good and faithful God. He is jealous of the priorities in our lives that get in the way of our relationship with Him.

Those "priorities" in our lives have become idols in our lives. Our families should not replace the Lord, nor should our jobs or our children's activities. Please hear my heart. I am not saying that those things are not important, but when you make your children go to school or you make yourself go to work and then, come Sunday, you talk yourself out of going to meet with the Lord because you "need a day to yourself" or "the kids need a break from their hectic week," you are making idols of what is keeping you from attending your church. Your relationship with the Lord is no longer the priority in your life.

Exodus 20:5 (NIV) says, "You shall not bow down to them or serve them, for I the Lord your God am a jealous God…" He is jealous for YOUR attention to Him! He wants a relationship with YOU above all things! We need to seek Him and His Kingdom first. Matthew 6:33 (NIV) says, "But seek first the kingdom of God and His righteousness, and all these things will be added unto you." Everything else will fall into place in every area of our lives if we will put Him first in all that we do.

Chapter 3: Hunger

Psalm 42:1

As the deer pants for streams of water,
so my soul pants for you, my God.

Psalms 27:8 (TPT) says this: "Lord, when You said to me, 'Seek My face,' my inner being responded, 'I'm seeking Your face with all my heart.'"

The few months leading up to revival, our church would have visitations of His presence during some of the Sunday morning services. For example, one Sunday morning service would be heavy with a sense of His Spirit, but it would be a few weeks later before we would experience that tangible presence again. Some of us wondered why it didn't happen every service. What did it take to have Him come and sit with us, to stay with us? What did it take to essentially host His presence? We were spiritually hungry for Him and for all He has for us.

Our pastor, Todd Smith, led us on a twenty-one day fast in January of 2018, several weeks before revival started. During this fast, our focus was seeking His face -- nothing more. We were not asking for handouts; we were not asking Him to do anything for us. We just wanted to see His face. We wanted realness. We wanted Him and Him alone. We were seeking Him simply for Who He *is* and not what He could do for us. We simply wanted Him in His fullness and glory.

Sometimes Christians don't pursue God directly or even at all. Sometimes Christians are content with just going to church on Sundays and maybe a mid-week service here and there. Maybe we have a fifteen-minute Bible reading in the morning or evening, but that's all the time we have for Him. Or maybe that's all we've been taught that we *need* to do. We are so busy with life that we leave God sitting in a chair in the corner. We attempt to do everything ourselves, without Him, until we've made a mess of things. Being the patient gentleman that He is, He waits on us to come into His presence, sit with Him, and spend time with Him. He waits for a true intimate relationship with us.

What exactly does it mean to seek His face? Seeking His face is seeking His presence. It is seeking to know Him and not just what He can do for us. It is not seeking Him for His handouts and His blessings. It is seeking Him and Him alone. It is seeking out His will and not ours. It is seeking His agenda and not ours. It is seeking Who He is. It is desiring to know Him. It is desiring to know His ways and His heart. It is desiring to be with Him, to spend time with Him. He is a Person! When you seek Him and Him alone, He will show up. There is nothing more that He wants other than for us to want Him enough to spend time with Him and devote our lives to Him.

The atmosphere changes when He walks into the room. You can sense His presence. There is an immediate reverence, awe, fear, and wonder that is nothing like anything else in this world. You simply know it is Him. Your heart and your spirit sense His presence and know automatically that it is the King of Kings, the Creator of your soul. There are many times when I walk into the sanctuary at church for prayer and immediately slow my walk because I can feel His presence. There is an awe in the atmosphere. There are days that you can feel His presence as soon as you pull into the parking lot. His presence changes everything within you and makes you want to Honor Him. He is the holy, powerful, almighty God.

The Lord has always wanted to be with us. The tabernacle in the Old Testament is a clear example of God wanting to "tabernacle" with His people. Tabernacle means a place of worship. Isn't it wonderful that even though we fell out of His presence in the Garden, He still made a way for us to fellowship with Him? He didn't leave us to fend for ourselves. He still wanted us even though we were not obedient. He still loves us and still wants to have a relationship with us even today. We have grieved Him so much, and yet He still passionately chases after us! What kind of god does that? Only the One who created us!

Spiritual hunger for the Lord is absolutely required for revival. In fact, I dare say that you cannot have revival without a profound hunger for His presence. His presence is everything! You have to want Him at all costs. You have to be willing to give up EVERYTHING for Him. Your soul has to pant for Him. There has to be an unwavering, unquenchable thirst and hunger for Him and His presence. Nothing else will satisfy you until you have His presence. Remember, it's all of you for all of Him.

Pastor Todd is always telling us to "die well," and those of us who serve and host the revival understand what he means. We know *why* we have to "die well." Holy Spirit cannot move if we are in the way! He cannot change us, purify us, cleanse us, teach us, train us, and use us if we keep getting in the way! We must yield to His wishes and let Him lead. We have to stop thinking that we know more than He does. We have to stop thinking that our ways are better than His. His plans are perfect! We are the created ones. It is time to put that selfish spirit away and line ourselves up with the Lord and what He wants to do. It is time to have HUNGER for Him, to put Him first in all that you do, and do what He wants. You have to die to the things that you want, period!

Smith Wigglesworth said, "The secret of spiritual success is a hunger that persists. It is an awful condition to be satisfied with one's spiritual attainments. God was and is looking for hungry, thirsty people."

Get hungry for who our Father is! Do not wait for tomorrow. If you were to die right now, would you want to stand before Him and tell Him you did not have time to spend with Him to learn who He is? Would you want to try to make an excuse as to why the entertainment of today's world was more important? He has all of eternity to listen to our excuses, but they will not get us anywhere. Wouldn't you prefer to hear, "Well done, good and faithful servant!" when you see Him?

I'm not saying you can't enjoy the ball game, TV show, or whatever else serves as your entertainment. But is it an idol in your life? Is your family an idol in your life? Do you put them above Him? What is keeping you from spending time with the Lord to learn who He is? GET HUNGRY FOR HIM! If you don't have hunger, ASK Him to make you hungry! He will do it.

He wants you to want Him! He is waiting for an invitation. Go ahead and ask Him now! Be honest with Him. Tell Him that you are sorry for not having a desire to know Him and who He is and what He is like. Ask Him to forgive you and to deposit a hunger for truth in your heart. Ask Him to open your eyes and heart to His wonders. Ask him to enable you to see things like He does. Ask Him to bring His Word alive to you as you open the pages of your Bible. Ask Holy Spirit to reveal His truth to you in your life. He will do it. I promise you won't regret asking Him!

Chapter 4: Revival Mess

Psalm 51:10

Create in me a clean heart, O God; and renew a right spirit within me.

Revival is hard and messy. Revival turns our hearts inside out, upside down, and cleans out all the "junk." And by junk, I mean all the crud that we have tried to deal with ourselves or even buried in half-hearted attempts to forget about them so that we don't have to deal with them. Revival is about making all the wrongs right. It's about repenting to others and especially to our Heavenly Father. It's about asking forgiveness from those whom you have wronged. It doesn't matter if you feel like they were the ones that hurt you or not. You still submit to Holy Spirit when He steps in and says, essentially, "No, I don't want that hurt buried. I want it brought to the surface. I need it out of the way, so let's deal with it now. Repent so that I can take you deeper in our relationship."

Repenting simply means asking Father for forgiveness. It means that you turn from that wicked way, whatever that was, and you seek the Lord and His ways. It means that whatever sin grieves the Father now grieves you. His presence makes you more aware of what grieves Him and what honors Him.

When revival came, it brought great repentance. I remember seeing people face down on the floor crying out in agony, while others were bent over at the waist with their hands outward, bowing in reverence. Others were literally running and shouting around the room like they had just won a once-in-a-lifetime trip around the world. Still others were kneeling at the altar or at their chair praying, crying, and worshiping Father. It wasn't as if Father was ministering to everyone all at once, either. His presence would come in waves, and it would affect each person differently. Some would be touched by the Lord during one service and not the next, but they would be ministered to in the one after that. It was simply Holy Spirit meeting each and every one of us in His perfect way and His perfect time. I also believe that He was giving us time to decide if we were going to give Him permission to cleanse our hearts before He would move us to the next step in the refining process. Those to whom the Lord was not ministering during a service would stay and intercede for those who were receiving from the Lord. Our hearts were being aligned with His to comfort, pray, and support each other.

Our tribe was being purified and strengthened.

You see, the Lord is a gentleman in the sense that He will not force you to love Him or to serve Him. He will not force you to follow Him. If you want to have your way, He will step back and let you have it. However, because of His goodness, He is waiting with open arms when we have made a mess of things to come running back to Him.

He rejoices when we come back to Him! Luke 15:3-7 says this, "Then Jesus told them this parable: "Suppose one of you has a hundred sheep and loses one of them. Doesn't he leave the ninety-nine in the open country and go after the lost sheep until he finds it? And when he finds it, he joyfully puts it on his shoulders and goes home. Then he calls his friends and neighbors together and says, 'Rejoice with me; I have found my lost sheep.' I tell you that in the same way there will be more rejoicing in Heaven over one sinner who repents than over ninety-nine righteous persons who do not need to repent." Do you see how Heaven rejoices over the one?

In revival, the Lord wants to change you. He wants to clear the muck so that His glory can shine through you. This is a difficult, messy process. Walking through the refining fire isn't easy. It is humiliating and humbling, to say the least. It literally takes dying to yourself and your wants. It requires your pride to be squashed and to become non-existent. It is all about Him and His glory. It is about His will, not ours. It is about His work, not ours. It is about His needs, not ours. It has now been over five years since the revival began, and the Lord still walks me through repentance and changes me daily. We cannot become "like Christ" overnight. Becoming like Christ requires walking with the Lord every day of our lives; it requires being eager for Him to mold us to be more like Him. This is a lifetime process, and it's ok that it takes that long!

Each and every day, the Lord will deal with something in my life. It may be my reaction to someone's driving that annoys me or that one coworker or boss that presses every button under the sun. It may be an old feeling of unworthiness that he wants me to leave at His feet once and for all. It may be words that an old high school friend said that still sting a little. It may be Holy Spirit teaching me to honor my husband a little more today than yesterday. It may be respecting and serving my husband better today than yesterday. It may be submitting to my husband's God-given authority over me and our household even though I don't want to (you have to squash the pride, remember?). It may be immediately forgiving a friend for a snide comment when my flesh wants to hold a grudge. It could be how the dog aggravates me when he barks for no reason for what seems like hours on end.

It truly doesn't matter what it is. If the Lord brings it to our attention, we must deal with it as He wishes. He truly wants to heal every wound in our hearts. He doesn't want old pains to hold us back or take our focus away from Him. He doesn't want us holding on to offenses. He wants to send His refining fire to the depths of our hearts and souls, dealing with the remnants of darkness. He wants to cleanse our hearts and souls, bringing healing. He wants to move us forward in that which He has in store for us.

When He sends His fire to us, we have a choice to make that change or not. I have a choice to let that one coworker push buttons or not. I have a choice to be my husband's helpmate, allowing him lead our home or not. See, the Lord has given me an option in every situation. I can respond in my flesh, or I can be obedient and take the matter to Him to see how He would have me respond. I can take all of those situations to Him and say, "Father, such and such happened today and honestly, I didn't respond in a positive way. I was offended, but I choose to not carry offense today. I forgive hurtful words and actions. I choose to give the matter to you. Please show me how You would respond. Help me to respond the way You would the next time I am faced with that situation. Help me to learn how to love the way You love. Help me to see the situation the way You see it. I choose to be obedient to Your Word and Your Word says _____ about how I should act."

Dig into His Word and see what it says about how you should act. He has given you all the tools you need. His Word will change you, but only if you will allow it.

When the North Georgia Revival first started, we spent the first three or four months on our faces, crying out for mercy and repenting to Father. The weight of His glory was so heavy that it left no room for debate. It seemed as if there were only two options: 1) stay in His presence and repent, allowing Him to change hearts; or 2) run out the door and not come back.

It was not easy to stay. It was very hard to confront and deal with the sin that Holy Spirit wanted to deal with. It wasn't like He was openly pointing the sin out to everyone, but it weighed on our individual hearts. Sometimes we repented to others as they prayed for us, and sometimes He was looking for a simple, silent repentance just to Him. It was different each and every time He manifested His presence in those early services of the revival.

I know many people who left our church permanently because they did not want revival. I think it is safe to say that about half of the people left! They said it was too hard to be there, and they were not ready to deal with what Father was asking them to deal with. Looking back, He was clearly walking us through His refining fire to purify us. We had to become spiritually clean and allow ourselves to be molded and shaped by His presence in order to be useable material for Him and His glory.

In my honest opinion, I would rather deal with the mess now, laying my pride aside, humbling myself, asking for His forgiveness. I would rather ask Him to change me now instead of continuing to waste my life not being in His will than to have to try to make excuses on Judgment Day! On that fateful, joyful, and mournful day, excuses will not mean anything. I do not want to disappoint Him by not fulfilling that which He created me to do.

Chapter 5: The Altar

Mark 8:35

For whoever wants to save their life will lose it, but whoever loses their life for Me and for the Gospel will save it.

You can't have revival without realizing the importance of the altar. The altar that I'm referring to isn't necessarily located in the church. It can be literally anywhere where you stop, acknowledge your sin, and seek His forgiveness. Sometimes it will feel like He spanked your bottom, but you must understand that Father truly knows and sees more than we can in this human form. He always wants to lovingly guide us in order to protect us from the spiritual things that this flesh and bone body cannot see.

About two months into my first year as a student of KINEO, I was driving home after class smoking a cigarette. When I first started smoking many years prior, it was just a social thing. Then I began to use smoking as a stress reliever. Eventually, smoking became a habit. I had tried quitting several times, but I was never successful. I always had an excuse to pick it back up, to give into the cravings. However, this night I began to feel remorseful about smoking.

In my car driving home that evening, I began to weep, feeling convicted that I was not treating my body as a temple for the Lord like I should have been (1 Corinthians 6:19). The Lord came into my car. His literal, *kavod* presence came into my car! I was trembling and so remorseful. I knew that smoking was a bad habit. Through tears, I told the Lord how sorry I was but that I couldn't quit. I had tried and had always failed. He very gently and lovingly told me, "You can do all things through Me." I immediately remembered the verse of Philippians 4:13. Again, through tears I said, "Lord, I will give up smoking right here and now. Please take away my cravings. I can't do this anymore on my own." And you know what? He did it! I have not smoked since, and I haven't had any symptoms of withdrawal at all!

Sometimes my flesh will try to talk me into having "just one" because I'm stressed, but I always remind my flesh that I gave smoking to the Lord and that I refuse to start again. I was delivered of an addiction that evening, and I am still smoke-free over five years later! All to HIS GLORY!

Don't try to take back what the Lord has delivered you from! If you do happen to give in, repent quickly and ask for His forgiveness. Ask for His help to make a better choice the next time you are faced with temptation. Don't beat yourself up about it. That's exactly what the enemy wants: condemnation. Holy Spirit will never condemn you! NEVER! Holy Spirit will bring conviction and give you a chance to repent.

The Lord gave me a choice that night. I had a choice to allow Him to correct me and help me or to back away and tell Him no. I found my altar that night. It was in His presence. Was it hard to quit? No, because He took away my cravings. Yes, because I did have to take action. I did have to choose to do His will. I had to choose to follow Him and give Him that habit. Remember, He is a gentleman. He will NEVER take anything from you! He will ask you to give it to Him, but it is always your choice to be obedient. He will always give you strength and grace for your journey.

During the first few months of the revival, each of us was constantly on our face. Each of us had to find our altar and deal with the things in our lives that the Lord wanted to deal with. We had to repent of whatever was in the way of the Lord being able to move. You must understand that He has His reasons for wanting you to let go of the garbage that is in your life. You can't see what He sees. Sometimes that garbage is legally preventing Him from moving in your life. We must live in a place of repentance so that we can stay close to Him. Sin separates us from Him. Also, anytime we dishonor Him, it grieves Him and pushes Him away. It hurts His heart! That's why repentance is so important. We must be in a position to carry more of His presence with us, and we can't do that if we are carrying tons of garbage and hardened hearts.

Even now, years into the revival, dying to self can be a daily struggle. Living in the altar space is hard. For example, it is almost a weekly struggle for me driving home from work on a Monday evening after staying at church late on Sunday serving at the revival. There's only so much coffee that will get you through the day! Many times I have wanted to drive right past the church, go home, and go to bed. However, my life doesn't belong to me, so I stop at the church for Monday corporate prayer.

I even made a reminder note with a label maker that is stuck to my dashboard just below the speedometer. It literally says, "Your life belongs to Him." That is all it needs to say. Every time I get in the car to head home from work, and I want to bypass the church, whether for prayer time or service, I am reminded that my life does not belong to me. It belongs to Him! He is worthy of my stopping by the church for an hour of prayer. He is worthy of my stopping by the church for the midweek service! HE IS WORTHY of my dying to myself, my wants, and my desires. He is worthy of my fighting this tired flesh to stay awake for one more hour to spend time with Him in corporate prayer. If it takes a sticky note plastered everywhere I go for the day to remind me to die to myself and live for Him, then that's what I'll do. It is so easy to get distracted today; that's exactly what the enemy wants. Our country and our families are in such a mess because we stopped putting the Lord first and started making church negotiable.

I used to have two original paintings hanging in my home. I had one hanging above each fireplace. I absolutely loved them, or at least I thought I did. They were hand-painted and were of two of my favorite childhood movies. The Lord asked me to get rid of them and began showing me the darkness that they represented. I still didn't want to get rid of them though. I knew the financial value of them, but they also held a special place in my heart. There was a stronghold there that I didn't realize; I wasn't really ready to confront it. Over the course of a couple of weeks, I managed to take them down and put them in a spare bedroom, but I still couldn't bring myself to get rid of them. I knew I wasn't supposed to sell them or give them away. Somehow, I knew the Lord wanted them destroyed. I just couldn't bring myself to do it.

The Lord is sometimes gracious in giving me time to process through the "whys." During this time, He taught me about spiritual doors and about how I was allowing demonic activity to have legal access in my home because of the items within my home. It wasn't necessarily the items themselves (although it very well can be the items themselves in a lot of cases) but more of what they represented and how it was exactly the opposite of the Lord. In fact, what they represented brought dishonor to the Lord, and it grieved Him.

I was sitting on my sofa one day by myself, when that revelation came to me. I heard the Lord say, "Am I not worth it?" My fanny jumped off that sofa and ran to the kitchen to grab the scissors out of the knife block so quickly that you would have thought my pants were on fire! I took the scissors and cut a gigantic X through the canvas of those two paintings! I declared that the stronghold they brought was broken off of me by the power of Jesus Christ and His authority. I put both of them in black trash bags and put them in the back of my car. I was at the trash dump the very next morning within minutes of their opening for business. It was such a blessing to be able to put the paintings into the trash chute and press the button for the compactor to start. I cannot explain the sense of relief I felt, and I know that the Lord was closing that spiritual door for me.

My husband and I went through every book, every music CD, every movie DVD, and every game in our home. We got rid of everything that was rated above a "G," and even most of those G-rated items were tossed in the trash as well. It was amazing to realize what we were allowing into our lives by having those items in our home. If it had any kind of violence in it, we tossed it. If there were any bad words or "brief" nudity, we tossed it. We even went so far as to think of the plot of the movie and asked ourselves if it honored the Lord or if it dishonored Him. If it didn't honor Him, then we tossed it. Even the movies that implied sin scenarios were tossed out. Now I'm not saying you have to go through your home and throw away all of your items, but for us, it was non-negotiable. We wanted to honor the Lord in everything, and we wanted more of His presence in our lives. We wanted anything that would even remotely grieve Him gone from our home as quickly as possible! The value of the items no longer meant anything to us. If we felt it dishonored Him, it was gone without any questions or hesitations.

We have to get back to a place of honoring the Lord in all that we do. Our spiritual survival depends on it. We cannot play with our faith any longer. We cannot co-mingle with the things that are blatantly disrespectful and dishonoring to the Lord. We cannot continue to allow wickedness on the basis of "it's just a movie; it's just a game; it's just this or that." We cannot be a clean, pure bride for Jesus Christ if we get entertainment from something that He died to save us from. We must become aware of the enemy that crouches at the door, ready to jump just as soon as we open that spiritual door. When that spiritual door is opened, we are giving the enemy legal access to wreak havoc in our lives. The Church must grow up and become the spiritual powerhouse it was meant to be!

I want to share a brief story I ran across recently. I don't know who the author is, so I cannot assign credit for the story. But it spoke to my heart. I hope it will be meaningful for you, as well:

The story of the Silversmith: "And he shall sit as a refiner and purifier of silver" (Malachi 3:3). This verse puzzled a Bible study group. One of the members offered to learn about the process of refining silver and inform them at their next study. He visited a silversmith and watched him at work. He watched the silversmith hold a piece of silver over the fire and let it heat up. The silversmith explained that in refining silver, you must hold the silver in the middle of the fire where the flames were hottest to burn away all the impurities. The member then thought about God holding us where the flames are the hottest to burn away our impurities. Then he thought again about the verse. "**And he shall sit as a refiner and purifier of silver**." He asked the silversmith if it was true that he had to **sit there** in front of the fire and watch the process at all times.

The silversmith answered that not only did he have to sit there holding the silver, but he had to keep his eyes on the silver the **entire time** it was tested in the fire. If the silver was left a moment too long in the flames, it would be destroyed. You must leave it long enough to serve the purpose, but not too long as it would destroy it. The member was silent for a moment. Then asked the silversmith, "**How do you know when silver is fully refined?**" He smiled and answered, "**Oh, that's easy — when I see my image in it**." (Author Unknown).

Father God must be first in each of our lives. He must be first above our families, our spouses, jobs, sports, everything. We need to get back to spending quality, daily time with Him. He truly longs to have a relationship with each one of us. After all, we were created to fellowship with Him! We must honor Him in all that we do, even when it means submitting to the Refiner's fire to rid ourselves of impurities. We can no longer make lame excuses for our relationship failures with Jesus Christ. He deserves everything from us. We must live in a place of repentance and reverence if we want more of Him in our lives.

I don't know about you, but I made a mess of my life when I was trying to do things my way. It was only when I submitted to Heavenly Father and His plans for my life that my life turned around. The things I was trying to accomplish on my own were no longer a struggle. Dreams were revitalized and the right doors began to open for me. Passion, love, laughter, and life came back into this dry, weary body. Joy came back into my life -- true joy that I had missed for so long and didn't even realize it was gone. I no longer hold back when I laugh, because God has taken away everything that was weighing me down!

Find your altar today and give Him everything. Let Him cleanse your heart and lead you to a place of true happiness, contentment, and trust. Work on building that relationship with Him daily. Make time for Him and let Him lead you into all the wonderful plans He has for your life.

Chapter 6: Holy Spirit

Matthew 3:11 NKJV

I indeed baptize you with water unto repentance, but He who is coming after me is mightier than I, whose sandals I am not worthy to carry. He will baptize you with the Holy Spirit and fire.

What happened to the body of Christ in the Western world? We, here in the West, have severely lacked the capability and desire to do the work of the Lord like the original disciples did. Generally speaking, we do not display that kind of power or boldness. What happened? How do we get back that level of faith and POWER that isn't broken if we are thrown into jail or beaten? What if we were threatened to be stoned if we didn't denounce Jesus? What if our family was threatened? Would we stand with boldness on our faith or buckle? Those are some pretty tough questions, aren't they? What choice would you make?

Holy Spirit is our answer. Well, technically the baptism in the

Holy Spirit is our answer. Stay with me; don't drop out here! In a very gentle, loving way (or a smack upside the head for those of us who are more hard-headed), I ask that you take off the religious goggles and ask the Lord to show you the truth of His Word. My step-dad told me a long time ago that "you can't believe one page of the Bible and not the other." At first it offended me because I was tied to a religious spirit. I didn't believe in that sort of thing. I was raised in a denominational church that didn't teach about this subject. I am very thankful I had the courage to ask Father to show me His truth.

Let's take a look at a few verses that talk about being filled with Holy Spirit:

Matthew 3:11 (NIV): "I baptize you with water for repentance. But after me comes one who is more powerful than I, whose sandals I am not worthy to carry. He will baptize you with the Holy Spirit and fire."

Mark 1:8 (NIV): "I baptize you with water, but He will baptize you with the Holy Spirit."

Luke 24:49 (NIV): "I am going to send you what my Father has promised; but stay in the city until you have been clothed with power from on high."

John 1:33 (NIV): "And I myself did not know Him, but the One who sent me to baptize with water told me, 'The man on whom you see the Spirit come down and remain is the One who will baptize with the Holy Spirit.'"

John 20:22 (NIV): "And with that he breathed on them and said, 'Receive the Holy Spirit.'"

Acts 1: 4-5 (NIV): "On one occasion, while He was eating with them, He gave them this command: 'Do not leave Jerusalem, but wait for the gift my Father promised, which you have heard Me speak about. For John baptized with water, but in a few days you will be baptized with the Holy Spirit.'"

Acts 2:4 (NIV): "And they were all filled with the Holy Spirit and began to speak with other tongues, as the Spirit was giving them utterance."

Acts 10:46 (NIV): "For they heard them speaking in tongues and praising God."

Acts 11:15-16 (NIV): "As I began to speak, the Holy Spirit came on them as He had come on us at the beginning. Then I remembered what the Lord had said: 'John baptized with water, but you will be baptized with the Holy Spirit.'"

Acts 19:1-6 (NIV): "While Apollos was at Corinth, Paul took the road through the interior and arrived at Ephesus. There he found some disciples and asked them, 'Did you receive the Holy Spirit when you believed?' They answered, 'No, we have not even heard that there is a Holy Spirit.' So Paul asked, 'Then what baptism did you receive?' 'John's baptism,' they replied. Paul said, 'John's baptism was a baptism of repentance. He told the people to believe in the one coming after him, that is, in Jesus.' On hearing this, they were baptized in the name of the Lord Jesus. When Paul placed his hands on them, the Holy Spirit came on them, and they spoke in tongues and prophesied."

Ephesians 6:18 (NIV): "And pray in the Spirit on all occasions with all kinds of prayers and requests. With this in mind, be alert and always keep on praying for all the Lord's people."

Jude 1:20-21 (NIV): "But you, dear friends, by building yourselves up in your most holy faith and praying in the Holy Spirit, keep yourselves in God's love as you wait for the mercy of our Lord Jesus Christ to bring you to eternal life."

Holy Spirit is a Person and part of the Trinity of God. Father God, Jesus Christ, and Holy Spirit are the full Trinity. They are three in one. Each of the Trinity has very distinct roles, but Holy Spirit is the most neglected. We lack the understanding of His importance in our lives. We lack the daily appreciation of His work in our lives and His daily ministry to us. We need to experience Him personally. When we do experience Him, it can't be described in human terms. We can try to explain it, but there just aren't any words. It is truly a supernatural experience and each person will experience Him differently.

Holy Spirit is the "Agent" of God on the Earth. We are His "host"! Holy Spirit is placed on the inside of us when we receive salvation. In fact, He is the One who seals our adoption into the body of Jesus Christ at salvation! He is not inferior to Father God or Jesus. He has a position of equality with Father and Jesus (the Son), and all three are equal in deity, nature, and essence.

Holy Spirit can be insulted, tested, resisted, and quenched. He can be grieved and forgotten. He reveals truth to us. He convicts us of our sin and prompts us for repentance, and essentially reveals Jesus and the Father's heart to us. He is the One who woos our soul and draws us to experience Salvation. Holy Spirit helps us pray in the Spirit when we need to pray the perfect will of the Father. Since our human minds don't always know what Father's perfect will is, praying in the Spirit will accomplish His will. Holy Spirit knows exactly what needs to be done, and He needs us to pray to accomplish it.

If you have never received the Baptism of Holy Spirit, with the evidence of speaking in tongues (praying in the Spirit), then I encourage you to ask Holy Spirit for it. It is not demonic, but in fact completely Biblical. Jesus's own mother spoke in tongues. In Acts 2:4 says, "All of them were filled with the Holy Spirit and began to speak in other tongues."

There are many great books on this topic. Here are a few that I read to answer the many questions I had:

* *Speaking in Tongues* and *He Sent Him* by Dr. Todd Smith

* *Holy Spirit: An Introduction* by John Bevere

* *The New You & The Holy Spirit* by Andrew Wommack

If you are still skeptical or scared, just ask the Lord to begin to reveal His truth to you. It is okay if it takes months of reading and researching the topic before you are ready to receive. I can certainly relate to that hesitation. I did my own research over a time period of about five months. I believe the Lord was peeling back one layer of truth at a time. He was allowing me to establish a firm foundation of truth before moving forward.

I also want to make a note that I was not one of those who immediately began speaking multiple words in tongues. I started out babbling like a baby in a new language. Essentially, that is what it is. It was a new language for me: my prayer language. As I began to pray more with my new language, I began hearing new words. My point here is this: don't let the enemy or your mind tell you that you're being foolish. It is real and you can do it. Your prayer language is yours and yours alone. No one else can mimic it and no one else can understand it with one exception. That exception is when the tongue and interpretation is given to edify the body of Christ. This usually happens in a corporate setting.

First Corinthians 14:2 (NLT) says this, "For if you have the ability to speak in tongues, you will be talking only to God, since people won't be able to understand you. You will be speaking by the power of the Spirit, but it will all be mysterious."

Go ahead and pray what comes through your spirit. You have a personal language that only your Heavenly Father can understand. Glory to God!

I believe revival has made me more aware of Holy Spirit and how he operates on the Earth. I have seen His power work to reconcile families, break addictions, and heal many sicknesses. However neat those things may be, the one that grabs my heart every time is when their relationship with Father is restored. So many believe that Father is mad at them. I also felt this way for a very long time. The truth is that He is always ready to receive the return of His prodigal children.

Look at this quote from Hudson Taylor: "Since the days of Pentecost, has the whole Church ever put aside every other work and waited upon Him for ten days, that the Spirit's power might be manifested? We give too much attention to method and machinery and resources, and too little to the source of power."

We have seen what God can do in our church services when we pray corporately for just an hour before every service. This time of praying releases the power of Holy Spirit. We are living in the midst of revival because we (our corporate body) are committed to fasting, praying, and seeking God's face for Him to move in our lives and in our church. Prayer moves our physical bodies out of the way so that we can focus on the Lord and what He wants us to do. Prayer is *the* most precious and most important time that we can spend with Him!

Chapter 7: Praying Heaven Down

1 Peter 4:7

The end of all things is near. Therefore be alert and of sober mind so that you may pray.

Why do we pray? Is there really a *need* to pray?

"The devil will try to stop you from praying because prayer stops him." –Reinhard Bonnke

"Prayer begets revival, which begets more prayer." –Jim Cymbala

"There has never been a spiritual awakening in any country or locality that did not begin in united prayer." –A. T. Pierson

Simply put, prayer changes things! It brings Heaven down to Earth. It moves mountains in our lives. It can change the outcome of almost any situation (as long as what we pray lines up with the will of Father). Prayer brings the will of the Lord into reality. It breaks strongholds in all areas of our lives and of the Church body. Prayer is one of our primary weapons!

The Church must pray! The Church must pray corporately, also. We know there is power in prayer. If we know this, then why don't we gather more often, with more and more people, and pray the will of the Father? Why is prayer not a priority for our own lives and for our churches and our Country? Our prayers move mountains! We need to pray MORE!

Jesus was our prototype and perfect example for everything we face in our daily lives. Let's take a look at His prayer life to see how important it was to Him.

Luke 3:21 (NIV): "Now when all the people were baptized, Jesus was also baptized, and while He was praying, Heaven was opened,"

Matthew 14:23 (NIV): "After He had sent the crowds away, He went up on the mountain by Himself to pray; and when it was evening, He was there alone."

Mark 6:46 (NIV): "After bidding them farewell, He left for the mountain to pray."

Luke 6:12 (NIV): "It was at this time that He went off to the mountain to pray, and He spent the whole night in prayer to God."

Mark 1:35 (NIV): "In the early morning, while it was still dark, Jesus got up, left the house, and went away to a secluded place, and was praying there."

Luke 5:16 (NIV): "But Jesus Himself would often slip away to the wilderness and pray."

Matthew 26:36 (NIV): "Then Jesus came with them to a place called Gethsemane, and said to His disciples, 'Sit here while I go over there and pray.'"

If Jesus spent so much time in prayer, why do we think we don't have to? I believe this is why the Church doesn't display the power of Holy Spirit today compared to the ground shaking power in the early Church. Jesus was all God in human form. He is our prototype. He spent countless hours in prayer and saw countless miracles. Many times, the Bibles says that "all" were healed when Jesus ministered to them. Could you imagine being able to heal *everyone* who was sick?

Did you know that the Moravian Brotherhood prayed twenty-four hours a day for one hundred years? Think about that for a moment and think about the lifestyle these people had. Think about what they had to give up in order to make that commitment. Think about those who woke in the middle of the night just because they committed themselves to get up and pray. Imagine the direction of our country and indeed the world if we as the Body of Christ would commit to praying like they did.

Our church spends five hours a week praying corporately. We have seen many miracles, healings, and life changes. We have seen marriages and families restored. We have seen people come in drunk and/or high on drugs and leave clear-headed and sober. Make no mistake though; prayer isn't about the miracles, and that is NOT what we ask and pray for. We seek His face and His presence. We pray for Him to keep us on our knees, on our faces, humbled, pure hearted, and holy before Him. We ask to keep our heart posture turned towards Him, to keep our eyes focused on Him, and to keep us at a place of quick repentance. We do not ask for anything from anyone. We simply want to see His Kingdom manifested here on the Earth and to host His presence until that glorious day of His return.

When Paul was in prison, there was an earthquake that shook the prison doors open. That earthquake was because of the group of people praying for his release from prison!

Look at the warning Peter gave us about prayer. 1 Peter 4:7 (NIV) says, "The end of all things is near. Therefore, be alert and of sober mind so that you may pray."

We are closer today to Jesus's return than at any other time in history. We must be able to pray the perfect will of God at all times. Our human minds cannot comprehend what His perfect will is at every moment but our spirits can. This is why it is so important for us to pray in the spirit as much as humanly possible.

Prayer must become the central ministry of the body of Christ. Remember that we do not battle with flesh and blood, but with powers and principalities. We pray and the Lord fights the battles for us. We must move in one accord with Holy Spirit. We must unite as ONE Body with ONE Spirit, and that ONE spirit is Holy Spirit! He will lead us to do the work of the Lord.

Ask Him today, right now, to begin to show you the truth of this. Ask for forgiveness so that He can have the legal authority to move in your life in this area. Be open-minded and ready to receive the revelation that He has for you. Stay hungry for all of Him.

Vance Havner put it this way: "It is not that God is stingy and must be coaxed, for He 'giveth liberally and upbraideth not.' It is that we ourselves are so shallow and sinful that we need to tarry before Him until our restless natures can be stilled and the clamor of outside voices be deadened so that we can hear His voice. Such a state is not easily reached, and the men God uses have paid a price in wrestlings and prevailing prayer. But it is such men who rise from their knees confident of His power and go forth to speak with authority."

Lord, may we tarry with You until we are in the midst of the greatest revival that this nation, and indeed the world, has ever seen! May we continue to pray Heaven down to Earth! May we continue to pray for Your Kingdom to come and Your will to be done here and now! May we remain steadfast and not grow weary! May we remain ever-focused on You! And may we be the generation that prepares the way for Your glorious return! Amen!

"When a Christian shuns fellowship with other Christians, the devil smiles. When he stops studying the Bible, the devil laughs. When he stops praying, the devil shouts for joy." – Corrie Ten Boom

"Every great movement of God can be traced to a kneeling figure." – Dwight L. Moody

"The prayer of the feeblest saint who lives in the Spirit and keeps right with God is a terror to Satan. The very powers of darkness are paralyzed by prayer; no spiritualistic séance can succeed in the presence of a humble praying saint. No wonder Satan tries to keep our minds fussy in active work til we cannot think in prayer." – Oswald Chambers

Chapter 8: God Is Always Good

Jeremiah 29:11 - 13

For I know the plans I have for you, declares the LORD, plans to prosper you and not to harm you, plans to give you hope and a future. Then you will call on me and come and pray to me, and I will listen to you. You will seek me and find me when you seek me with all your heart.

One of the cornerstones of the Christian faith is that Father God is always good. If we lack the basic understanding and acceptance of this, we will crumble under the weight of every battle and every circumstance. We may even begin to question God due to a lack of understanding of Who He is and what our faith is primarily built upon.

I have been a Christian since I was nine years old. I accepted Jesus Christ as my Savior in a small-town denominational church. I remember feeling a stirring on the inside of me that prompted me to move at an offer to accept Jesus Christ as my Lord and Savior. Even though joy was there as well as the desire to please the Lord, I did not have a true understanding of what I owed to Him and what belonged to me in my covenant. To an extent, my childish mind thought I was getting a "get out of hell free" card. I did not have a firm foundation on which to grow.

I am not saying the offers for discipleship were not there; I am sure they were. It is more likely that I was not interested in them. I was a child and simply did not understand what my responsibility for salvation was. I enjoyed Sunday School but it just wasn't enough to build a foundation for me. However, when KINEO Ministry Training Center became an opportunity for me, I jumped in. This Biblical teaching has given me the foundation that I so desperately needed in my life. It has taught me who God really is, what He did for me, who I am in Him, and what belongs to me because of Jesus's sacrifice on the cross.

Having this foundation has brought me the greatest peace in some of the hardest storms I have faced in my life. In January 2021, I found my beloved aunt deceased. The circumstances were horrific and I struggled for many months trying to understand and adjust to not having her in my life. She was more than an aunt to me. She and I had grown quite close since my grandmother passed away a few years prior. We talked multiple times a day so it was a hard adjustment for me to learn how to live without my beloved friend.

Father God doesn't make or let bad things happen to bring punishment to us. Bad things happen because of the fallen world we live in. If we allow God to move in our lives, He will restore all that has been lost. He will heal our heartache and restore the joy in our lives. Trusting Him is the only way to live this life here in this fallen world.

Remember that He sees and knows things that we cannot possibly know or comprehend. It is our responsibility as His children to trust in the only One who can lead, guide, and protect us. If we are living outside of the Father's will in our lives, then we are outside of His divine, legal protection! Do not hold Him responsible for something that He does not have legal authority over. Please do not misunderstand. Every bad thing that happens isn't always because of sin or because we aren't in the will of the Father. My point here is that we are to TRUST HIM with everything we have. We have to trust that He has greater plans for us than we can possibly imagine.

In November 2021, my unborn grandson was diagnosed with Congenital Diaphragmatic Hernia (CDH). From the time of diagnosis until the time of birth in May 2022, we fasted and prayed with our prayer warriors from our class tribe. We believed and prayed diligently for a complete healing for baby Oliver. We prayed for a great group of doctors to care for him, and for the Lord to carry us and to guide our family along the journey.

Just as church was letting out one Sunday, we got a phone call that we never thought we would receive. Twenty days after Oliver's birth, we had to say goodbye to our sweet baby. It was not only the most painful day of my life but also the most painful day in the life of my family. We expected complete healing here on the Earth, and we were prepared to continue fasting and praying during the long journey.

Living in the midst of revival, I never had a doubt that Oliver would live. I never doubted that he would be healed and would be running around playing with his big sister one day. I truly thought it would be a long healing process. We had hunkered down during the pregnancy and prayed constantly, declaring and decreeing our covenant with Father and claimed the healing that belonged to us. We were ready to continue fighting for his healing after his birth. We never imagined that it would be a short twenty days instead.

Even though Oliver is not here with us, I know he is with our Father. He is healed, whole, and perfect. We have Jesus's promise that we will spend eternity together in Heaven. Oliver is waiting on us to get to there! I have zero doubt that he will be at those glorious gates the moment we arrive in Heaven. We will get to spend eternity with him. It is hard only for a short time when you think about how long forever really is.

No matter what happens in your life, you must hold on to the fact that God is good! He is always good no matter what! God did not cause Oliver's medical problems, nor did He create them so that we could go through such heartache and loss. We live in a fallen world and sometimes things like this happen. Sometimes miracles happen and sometimes they don't. Sometimes healings happen and sometimes they don't. It's not my place to judge Father God, nor is it my place to question why it didn't go the way I thought it would. It is not my place to assume that I know more than Father or that my way is better than His.

I do not blame God for Oliver's death. Our Creator, Father God, is the Author of life! Father God can be nothing but good. It is His very nature! He cannot be anything else. Faith is practiced by trusting in Him and His promises. Placing my faith and trust in Him, and Him alone, is what gets me through every day, but especially the tough days. I don't know why God didn't heal our sweet Oliver, but I don't have to know. All I need to know is that

Jesus has him, and I'll see him again one day soon. My Father in Heaven knows exactly what He is doing, and it is not my place to question Him. I am *His* creation, and it is my place to learn to trust in Him and to trust that He ALWAYS has the best plan!

Father God gets so much blamed on Him because we do not know His Word. We don't know who He is because we're too busy doing other things and do not spend enough time with Him getting to know who He is. It is truly heartbreaking to think about how much I blamed Him throughout my life when I should have been blaming myself for my poor choices (and the consequences of those choices) or blaming the enemy. I am grateful that I have grown in my spiritual maturity and that I can declare in every circumstance that **God is good**!

We should always keep our eyes on Jesus, no matter if we are in the valley or on the mountain. If we keep our focus on Him, He will always lead the way. He will always be there to comfort us and to guide us. He will lead us through every storm, and we will come out stronger and better than we were before the storm. He never promised we wouldn't have storms in our lives, but He did promise that He wouldn't leave us. That means that He will walk through the storm with us and help us grow and mature. Your storm is always a testimony and should be used to help someone else who has gone through something similar. Never doubt God's goodness and how He brought you out of your storm.

I want to encourage you to spend time with the Lord daily reading His Word. It will not only build your faith but it will build a foundation for you to stand on when the storms come. The storms of life *will* come, and you need to be prepared for them. If you do not have a firm foundation to stand upon, which includes a dedicated prayer life, that storm is going to knock the wind out of you and you may be picking up the pieces for a long time. It is time to learn what belongs to you in your covenant with the Lord and build your foundation. The first step in this is to know beyond a shadow of a doubt that our Heavenly Father is always good. It is His very nature.

There is always light in the storm and that light is Jesus. Stay focused on Him and build your foundation on Him. Ask Him what it is that you need to learn during the storm. Don't focus on the storm. Focus on Him! Get into His Word and learn about Him. The world is growing darker, but it is in the darkness that the light of Jesus shines brighter and brighter!

Chapter 9: Your Authority in Him

Ephesians 6:11-12

Put on the full armor of God, so that you can take your stand against the devil's schemes. For our struggle is not against flesh and blood, but against the rulers, against the authorities, against the powers of this dark world and against the spiritual forces of evil in the Heavenly realms.

When we were first invited to Christ Fellowship Church, I would wake up almost every Sunday morning with a migraine headache. My husband and I would go to our chiropractor on Saturday for an adjustment so that I wouldn't have a headache the following day. It never failed though. I would still wake up with one. They were so bad and painful that it would make me sick. Therefore, we would stay home and miss church.

One Sunday morning my husband called his mom. He told her that I had another headache and we were not going to meet them at church. She began to pray in the Spirit. A few moments later she told him that it was a demonic attack. He needed to put his hands on my head and command the devil and his schemes to flee. My headache left within a few minutes! I still have a migraine about once or twice a year but the weekly, Sunday morning attacks have stopped.

This was my first encounter with authority. I did not realize that, though, until a few years later. I had been having nightmares for quite a few years. The very first one I woke up to an ice-cold room. I had awakened because I felt like someone had their hands on my throat choking me. I woke up gasping for air. I could still feel the pressure on my throat. I truly thought I was going crazy.

Every few months I would have another nightmare. Most of them felt as if they were pulling my spirit down to hell. I would be gripped with unimaginable, indescribable fear. I would begin speaking the name of Jesus with just the slightest whisper until I felt like I was released. I would then wake up and fight with fear, anxiety, and depression for months and months. My husband was the greatest person on the planet praying for me and speaking protection over me during this time. This literally went on for several years. I was too scared to tell anyone other than my husband. I was afraid people would think I was crazy.

In one of my KINEO classes, we began studying our authority. We had already learned about the covenant we were in with Father God. In this class we were learning our authority that we have because of our covenant. The next nightmare I had, I instantly and subconsciously used that authority! When I felt my spirit being pulled down and the darkness surrounding me again, I gave the COMMAND for them to release me in the name of Jesus. This time was different. I didn't speak Jesus until He came to my rescue. I used the authority that Jesus gave me in my covenant, and I commanded them to release me. Praise God that that was the last nightmare I've had!

There is something to be said when you learn your authority in Christ Jesus. Boldness and confidence step in. You know who you are in Him. You know who He is in you. You learn that the devil and his minions are nothing to you. They have no authority over you. They are powerless. They are nothing. They cannot harm you. They are beneath you. Jesus defeated death, hell, and the grave when He died on the cross for us. Guess what? Jesus is IN you! That means that those pesky demons are defeated in your life because Jesus is in you! You have all authority over the darkness because of Jesus and his sacrifice!

Grasp ahold of everything that Jesus has done for you. He has conquered ALL! He is risen! He reigns! His grave is the ONLY grave that is empty. He is the only one who died, went to hell, took back the keys (authority that Adam lost), and walked the Earth before ascending to Heaven. He ascended to Heaven so that He could put His blood on the Mercy Seat and cover our sins once and for all! He has conquered ALL! There is not one single thing that His blood doesn't cover. There is no sin that His blood will not cover. Because of His victory over death, hell, and the grave, we have full authority over it, too. Give Him praise for His victory!

Living in the midst of this revival, I have witnessed a few manifestations and deliverances. Prior to the revival, this southern girl thought that kind of stuff only happened in the movies. However, you cannot "un-see" something that you have witnessed on more than one occasion. The first thing I ever noticed while witnessing this was the verbal authority being used. There truly is power and authority in Christ Jesus.

No matter what spiritual door we have opened to the enemy, we have the authority to close it. Spend time in His Word every day and study it. Put on the full armor of God from Ephesians 6 and the devil will flee from you. You will have tests and storms in your life but you have the power and authority to endure and overcome them.

Your soul is extremely valuable. Heaven and Hell both want it. Think about that for a few minutes. Hell will do everything possible to keep you from getting closer to Father. The devil will literally torment you trying to get you back into his playground. He will do everything, including trying to kill you, to keep you from fulfilling your purpose.

If the devil is leaving you alone, then he does not see you as a threat. Make the decision today that you will seek Father with all of your heart. Take the time to learn all that Jesus has done for you. You will then know what authority you have in Him. Having this newfound revelation of your identity and authority is a weapon. You will have full confidence when the enemy comes at you. You will know exactly what you can do about it and how to stop him.

Never forget that the One who created you is the One who hung on a cross for you! That is how much your Heavenly Father loves you! You were worth Him dying for! Realizing all that He has done for you softens your heart and brings you to a place of gratitude. When gratefulness comes, it brings a whole, new level of praise, worship, obedience, and relationship. Operating from a position of gratitude in all that we do is very powerful. It is a weapon the enemy cannot comprehend.

Acts 19:13-16 tells a story of several people casting out demons using Jesus's authority, but the outcome did not go so well.

"Some Jews who went around driving out evil spirits tried to invoke the name of the Lord Jesus over those who were demon-possessed. They would say, 'In the name of Jesus whom Paul preaches, I command you to come out.' Seven sons of Sceva, a Jewish chief priest, were doing this. One day the evil spirit answered them, 'Jesus I know, and Paul I know about, but who are you?' Then the man who had the evil spirit jumped on them and overpowered them all. He gave them such a beating that they ran out of the house naked and bleeding."

The demons *knew* who Paul was. That tells me that Paul operated in the authority and power of Jesus so much that the demons recognized him by name! An unbeliever can use the power and authority of Jesus's name but the difference is *knowing* the One whose power we stand on and operate in. Paul spent a lot of time in prayer and knew exactly where and Who this authority came from.

You receive that power and authority the minute you become a Believer. However, you must know what belongs to you in your covenant. You must study His Word. You must spend time getting to know the One, or you may be the one running out the door bleeding and without your clothes.

Authority exercised with humility, and obedience accepted with delight are the very lines along which our spirits live.

- C.S. Lewis

Afterword

It is my prayer that what I have shared in this book will bring you to one point and one point only. That point is to love and honor Jesus with all that you are and all that you do. He gave up everything to come in human form to redeem us. He loved us so much that He was willing to do that! He saw you and me on this side of the cross. His work on the cross has redeemed us so that our full access to Him and Father has been restored. He is worthy of our love, respect, obedience, and honor.

I know that there is a lot of religious debate on speaking in tongues, the cessation of the gifts of the Holy Spirit, *et cetera*. Even if we do not agree on these items, I am asking you to seek the Lord with all your heart. If you are not hungry for Him, ask Him to increase your hunger. If you don't believe something in His Word, ask Him to increase your faith and to show you His truth. That's what I did. I spent months reading and researching for myself.

I had been taught that certain things weren't true, they "don't happen today," or they were "only for the original twelve disciples." I was at a point in my life where I wanted to know and read for myself instead of relying on someone else's knowledge or experience. I was hungry for His truth. I was not going to stop until I discovered every bit of truth that I was after. I wanted to know that the God in the Old Testament was and is the same powerful God of the New Testament. I wanted to know without a doubt that Father is the same yesterday, today, and forever. I had to open my mind to believe every page of His Word. I had to repent for not believing all of His Word.

All of God isn't in the Bible but the Bible is all about God. If everything about God could fit in the Bible, He wouldn't be God. We have to take control of our thoughts and realize that we cannot understand someone so great and powerful as our Creator. We shouldn't even try! Pride can sneak in when we think we know more than our Creator does.

To protect yourself when seeking the truth, always pray for His protection. A simple prayer such as this will provide all the protection you need: *Father, I come to you hungry for ALL of your truth. I refuse to settle for anything less than all of You. Father, I ask that you open my eyes and my heart to see your truth. I repent for not believing in ____ and ask that You show me the truth. Thank You for protecting me from any evil that lurks at the door. I repent for any of my sins and ask for Your forgiveness. Lord, I repent if there is even an*

ounce of a modern-day Pharisee within me. Lord, I want to see you in
all that You are. Lord, thank You for protecting me while I search for
truth. Thank You for opening my heart and preparing my heart and
my mind to receive Your truth.

I pray that you have the kind of hunger that consumes you in a healthy way! I pray that you rise early in the mornings for your quiet time with Him and that you do it eagerly and with expectation while spending quality time with Him.

Matthew 7:21-23 says this: "Not everyone who says to Me, 'Lord, Lord,' will enter the kingdom of Heaven, but only the one who does the will of my Father who is in Heaven. Many will say to Me on that day, 'Lord, Lord, did we not prophesy in Your name and in Your name drive out demons and in Your name perform many miracles?' Then I will tell them plainly, 'I never knew you. Away from Me, you evildoers!'"

Do you know Him? Do you truly know how much He loves you? Do you know what grieves Him? Do you know what brings Him joy? Do you know the multiple ways we can worship Him? Do you know how to honor Him? Do you really know Him like you know your best friend or spouse?

I want to encourage you to live life in a constant state of

Him and His presence in your life. Always be aware

s. Always honor those around you. Honoring them

⌐rings honor to Him. Love on those around you. That honors Him, too. If you lack any of the fruit of the Spirit, ask the Lord to change you and to help you grow in that area. Then listen for His guidance.

I want to encourage you to be the Christian that represents Jesus well. Don't be the one that lives in sin every day and makes no effort to change. You did not receive a "get out of hell free" card. Live your life with your nose to the floor humbly in prayer. Repent of any sin quickly, especially at the prompting of Holy Spirit. Remember, He will bring conviction, not condemnation. Ask the Lord to help you make the correct decision or take the correct action the next time you are faced with the same or similar situation. Holy Spirit is your Helper. He will help you whenever you ask according to His Word!

The Lord has given us all that we need to live a sanctified life. It won't happen overnight, so don't be too hard on yourself. The key is to listen for Holy Spirit and to repent as quickly as we hear His voice or as soon as we realize it. We won't get it right every time and that's okay. This is a life-long learning process. No one is perfect. We will all miss something somewhere. The important thing is that we repent and do it promptly. We are to go from glory to glory to glory. Repenting of our sin allows Him to continue to move in our lives.

I want to touch on one more topic and that is the topic of unity in the body of Christ. We must get to a place where we support and honor those of the same faith even among different denominations. This disunity has created weakness in the body of Christ for centuries! Let us be the ones who end the strife between denominations and, instead, find a way to lock arms and place our focus on Jesus. One of His commissions to us was to love one another.

How can we continue to try to save souls when we can't even get along amongst ourselves as members of different denominations? It pains me to see one denomination poking fun at another. I can only imagine how disappointed the Lord must be as He sees us bickering amongst each other. We should be praying for each other as brothers and sisters of Christ Jesus. Instead, we are taking Satan's bait and creating disunity in the body of Christ. How very shameful and foolish of the Church to be caught up in this behavior.

Forgive us, Lord! Bring unity to Your Church, Jesus!

My final prayer is that you will do all that you can to get to know Him more, to honor Him in all that you do, to stay humble and broken before Him in reverential fear and awe, and to love Him well.

Much love and many blessings to you!

About The Author

Michelle Lamb was raised in a denominational church. She gave her life to Christ as a child, but never developed a relationship with the Lord. She had always questioned the accuracy of the Bible in her mind and if she was really "saved." Why did God display so much power then and not now? Where was the God of the Bible? Why was He so present and powerful in the Bible stories but not now? How do we really know that those stories are true?

One day she received an invitation from her mother-in-love and sister-in-love to visit a non-denominational church. This church had a ministry training center that would change her life.

Michelle enrolled in **KINEO** Ministry Training Center and the Lord began to work on her from the very first class. Within a few weeks, she found herself overwhelmed by the evidence and truth. She made a decision that she would live the rest of her life honoring the Lord. She finally had the foundation of truth she desperately needed. This truth transformed her life and walk with Jesus.

The North Georgia Revival started during her first year at the Ministry Training Center. The encounter she had with Jesus in the water **marked** her forever. Living in the midst of revival has had a profound impact on her daily walk with the Lord. It has taught her how to honor and host the presence of the Lord in every aspect of her life and how to carry the seed of revival.

Michelle and her husband, Jason, have faithfully served at the North Georgia Revival since it began in February, 2018. Michelle enjoys spending time with her growing family, serving the Lord, and writing. She has a passion for coaching others to financial freedom and optimal health.

Made in the USA
Columbia, SC
17 October 2023